To Lily + L
I hope you enjoy this
Love + xx's
Melanie

The Kitten's
Garden of Verses

Oliver Herford

THE KITTEN'S GARDEN OF VERSES.

Oliver Herford

The Kitten's Garden
of Verses

By

Oliver Herford

New York · Charles Scribner's Sons
1911

BOOKS BY OLIVER HERFORD

WITH PICTURES BY THE AUTHOR

PUBLISHED BY CHARLES SCRIBNER'S SONS

THE BASHFUL EARTHQUAKE

A CHILD'S PRIMER OF NATURAL HISTORY

OVERHEARD IN A GARDEN

MORE ANIMALS

THE RUBAIYAT OF A PERSIAN KITTEN

THE FAIRY GODMOTHER-IN-LAW

A LITTLE BOOK OF BORES

THE PETER PAN ALPHABET

THE ASTONISHING TALE OF A PEN-AND-INK PUPPET

A KITTEN'S GARDEN OF VERSES

WITH JOHN CECIL CLAY

CUPID'S CYCLOPEDIA

CUPID'S FAIR-WEATHER BOOKE

To HAFIZ

Contents

Winter and Summer

In Winter when the air is chill,
     And winds are blowing loud and shrill,
All snug and warm I sit and purr,
     Wrapped in my overcoat of fur.

In Summer quite the other way,
     I find it very hot all day,
But Human People do not care,
     For they have nice thin clothes to wear.

And does it not seem hard to you,
     When all the world is like a stew,
And I am much too warm to purr,
     I have to wear my Winter Fur?

Rain

The rain is raining everywhere,
    Kittens to shelter fly—
But Human Folk wear overshoes,
    To keep their hind paws dry.

The Shadow Kitten

There's a funny little kitten that tries to look like me,
  But though I'm round and fluffy, he's as flat as flat can be;
And when I try to mew to him he never makes a sound,
  And when I jump into the air he never leaves the ground.

He has a way of growing, I don't understand at all.
  Sometimes he's very little and sometimes he's very tall.
And once when in the garden when the sun came up at dawn
  He grew so big I think he stretched half-way across the lawn.

Education

When People think that Kittens play,
        It's really quite the other way.
For when they chase the Ball or Bobbin
        They learn to catch a Mouse or Robin.

The Kitten, deaf to Duty's call,
        Who will not chase the bounding ball,
A hungry Cathood will enjoy,
        The scorn of Mouse and Bird and Boy.

A Thought

It's very nice to think of how
    In every country lives a Cow
To furnish milk with all her might
    For Kittens' comfort and delight.

The Lion

The Lion does not move at all,
     Winter or Summer, Spring or Fall,
He does not even stretch or yawn,
     But lies in silence on the lawn.

He must be lazy it is plain,
     For there is moss upon his mane,
And what is more, a pair of Daws
     Have built a nest between his paws.

Oh, Lazy Lion, big and brown,
This is no time for lying down!
The Sun is shining, can't you see?
Oh, please wake up and play with me.

The Milk Jug

The Gentle Milk Jug blue and white
  I love with all my soul,
She pours herself with all her might
  To fill my breakfast bowl.

All day she sits upon the shelf,
  She does not jump or climb—
She only waits to pour herself
  When 'tis my supper-time.

And when the Jug is empty quite,
  I shall not mew in vain,
The Friendly Cow, all red and white,
  Will fill her up again.

Happy Thought

The world is so full of a number of Mice
I'm sure that we all should be happy and nice.

Kitten's Night Thought

When Human Folk put out the light,
    And think they've made it dark as night,
A Pussy Cat sees every bit
    As well as when the lights are lit.

When Human Folk have gone upstairs,
    And shed their skins and said their prayers,
And there is no one to annoy,
    Then Pussy may her life enjoy.

No Human hands to pinch or slap,
    Or rub her fur against the nap,
Or throw cold water from a pail,
    Or make a handle of her tail.

And so you will not think it wrong
    When she can play the whole night long,
With no one to disturb her play,
    That Pussy goes to bed by day.

The Puncture

When I was just a Kitten small,
    They gave to me a Rubber Ball
To roll upon the floor.
    One day I tapped it with my paw
And pierced the rubber with my claw;
    Now it will roll no more.

Good and Bad Kittens

Kittens, you are very little,
> And your kitten bones are brittle,
If you'd grow to Cats respected,
> See your play be not neglected.

Smite the Sudden Spool, and spring
> Upon the Swift Elusive String,
Thus you learn to catch the wary
> Mister Mouse or Miss Canary.

That is how in Foreign Places
> Fluffy Cubs with Kitten faces,
Where the mango waves sedately,
> Grow to Lions large and stately.

But the Kittencats who snatch
> Rudely for their food, or scratch,
Grow to Tomcats gaunt and gory,—
> Theirs is quite another story.

Cats like these are put away
    By the dread S. P. C. A.,
Or to trusting Aunts and Sisters
    Sold as Sable Muffs and Wristers.

Anticipation

When I grow up I mean to be
A Lion large and fierce to see.
I'll mew so loud that Cook in fright
Will give me all the cream in sight.
And anyone who dares to say
"Poor Puss" to me will rue the day.
Then having swallowed him I'll creep
Into the Guest Room Bed to sleep.

Foreign Kittens

Kittens large and Kittens small,
Prowling on the Back Yard Wall,
Though your fur be rough and few,
I should like to play with you.
Though you roam the dangerous street,
And have curious things to eat,
Though you sleep in barn or loft,
With no cushions warm and soft,

16

The Kitten's Garden of Verses

Though you have to stay out-doors
When it's cold or when it pours,
Though your fur is all askew —
How I'd like to play with you!

The Joy Ride

When Mistress Peggy moves around,
　　Her dresses make a mocking sound.
"You can't catch me!" they seem to say—
　　I often steal a ride that way.

Facilis Ascensus

Up into the Cherry Tree,
　　Who should climb but little me,
With both my Paws I hold on tight,
　　And look upon a pleasant sight.

There are the Gardens far away,
　　Where little Foreign Kittens play,
And those queer specks of black and brown
　　Are naughty cats that live in Town.

And there among the tulips red,
     Where I may never lay my head,
I see the Cruel Gardener hoe
     The baby weeds that may not grow.

Now I climb down—"Oh dear,"—I mew,
     "Which end goes first—what shall I do?
Oh, good Kind Gardener, big and brown,
     Please come and help this Kitten down."

The Whole Duty of Kittens

When Human Folk at Table eat,
    A Kitten must not mew for meat,
Or jump to grab it from the Dish,
    (*Unless it happens to be fish*).

The Outing

My Bed is like a little Bark,
    The hatch is battened down,
And in the basket cabin dark
    I sail away from Town.

Now, when they lift the lid, a scene
    Of wonder meets my eyes,
Tall waving Feather-Dusters green,

22

The Kitten's Garden of Verses

That seem to touch the skies.

And over all the Ground is spread
    A Rug of Emerald sweet
Most deep enough to hide my head
    And tickly to my feet.

And here's the Cow, calm-eyed stands she,
    The Genie of the Jug,
Beneath the Feather-Duster Tree,
    And eats the Emerald Rug.

The Puppy

The Puppy cannot mew or talk,
    He has a funny kind of walk,
His tail is difficult to wag
    And that's what makes him walk zigzag.

He is the Kitten of a Dog,
    From morn till night he's all agog—
Forever seeking something new
    That's good but isn't meant to chew.

He romps about the Tulip bed,
    And chews the Flowers white and red,
And when the Gardener comes to see
    He's sure to blame mamma or me.

One game that cannot ever fail
> To please him is to chase his tail—
(To catch one's tail, 'twixt me and you,
> Is not an easy thing to do.)

If he has not a pretty face
> he Puppy's heart is in its place.
I'm sorry he must grow into
> A Horrid, Noisy Dog, aren't you?

The Moon

The Moon is like a big round cheese
        That shines above the garden trees,
And like a cheese grows less each night,
        As though some one had had a bite.

The Mouse delights to nibble cheese,
        The Dog bites anything he sees—
But how could they bite off the Moon
        Unless they went in a balloon?

And Human People, when they eat
     They think it rude to bite their meat,
They use a Knife or Fork or Spoon;
     Who is it then that bites the moon?

The Golden Cat

Great is the Golden Cat who treads
        The Blue Roof Garden o'er our heads,
The never tired smiling One
        That Human People call the Sun.

He stretches forth his paw at dawn
        And though the blinds are closely drawn
His claws peep through like Rays of Light,
        To catch the fluttering Bird of Night.

The Kitten's Garden of Verses

He smiles into the Hayloft dim
> And the brown Hay smiles back at him,
And when he strokes the Earth's green fur
> He makes the Fields and Meadows purr.

His face is one big Golden smile,
> It measures round, at least a mile—
How dull our World would be, and flat,
> Without the Golden Pussy Cat.

An Inquiry

A Birdie cocked his little head,
    Winked his eye at me and said,
"Say, are you a Pussy Willer,
    Or just a Kitty-Catty pillar?"

A Kitten's Fancy

The Kitten mews outside the Door,
    The Cat-bird in the Tree,
The Sea-mew mews upon the Shore,
    The Catfish in the Sea.

The Emu with his feathers queer
    Is mewing in the Zoo.
Why is it that I never hear
    A Pussy-willow mew?

In Darkest Africa

At evening when the lamp is lit,
    The tired Human People sit
And doze, or turn with solemn looks
    The speckled pages of their books.

Then I, the Dangerous Kitten, prowl
    And in the Shadows softly growl,
And roam about the farthest floor
    Where Kitten never trod before.

And, crouching in the jungle damp,
    I watch the Human Hunter's camp,
Ready to spring with fearful roar

The Kitten's Garden of Verses

As soon as I shall hear them snore.

And then with stealthy tread I crawl
        Into the dark and trackless hall,
Where 'neath the Hat-tree's shadows deep
        Umbrellas fold their wings and sleep.

A cuckoo calls—and to their dens
        The People climb like frightened hens,
And I'm alone—and no one cares
        In Darkest Africa—down stairs.

The Dog

The Dog is black or white or brown
        And sometimes spotted like a clown.
He loves to make a foolish noise
        And Human Company enjoys.

The Human People pat his head
        And teach him to pretend he's dead,
And beg, and fetch and carry too;
        Things that no well-bred Cat will do.

34

At Human jokes, however stale,
      He jumps about and wags his tail,
And Human People clap their hands
      And think he really understands.

They say "Good Dog" to him. To us
      They say "Poor Puss," and make no fuss.
Why Dogs are "good" and Cats are "poor"
      I fail to understand, I'm sure.

To Someone very Good and Just,
      Who has proved worthy of her trust,
A Cat will *sometimes* condescend—
      The Dog is Everybody's friend.

The Game

Watching a ball on the end of a string,
    Watching it swing back and to,
Oh, I do think it the pleasantest thing
    Ever a Kitten can do.

First it goes this way, then it goes that,
    Just like a bird on the wing.
And all of a tremble I crouch on the mat
    Like a Lion, preparing to spring.

The Kitten's Garden of Verses

And now with a terrible deafening mew,
Like a Tiger I leap on my prey,
And just when I think I have torn it in two
It is up in the air and away.

Lightning Source UK Ltd.
Milton Keynes UK
UKHW011247080221
378426UK00001B/96

9 781406 586183